CREDIT
REPAIR SECRETS

Learn How To Fix Your Bad Credit
With Strategies To Raise Your Credit Score,
Overcome Debt, And Protect
Your Financial Life

BRAD KENTEN

Table Of Contents

INTRODUCTION **6**

CHAPTER 1: HOW TO START AND HOW IT WORKS................... **8**

GETTING STARTED CLEANING UP YOUR CREDIT—THE DEBT SNOWBALL....... 8

WHAT SHOULD YOU INCLUDE IN YOUR DEBT SNOWBALL?........................... 11

IS CREDIT REPAIR ETHICAL? 12

THE WARNING SIGNS WHEN CHOOSING A CREDIT REPAIR COMPANY 13

CHAPTER 2: WHAT TO KNOW ABOUT CREDIT **16**

15 THINGS TO KNOW ABOUT CREDIT 16

WHAT IS A GOOD CREDIT SCORE? 22

UNDERSTANDING CREDIT SCORES 26

BUSINESS CREDIT SCORES 27

CHAPTER 3: SECTION 609 AND FCRA **30**

WHAT IS SECTION 609? 30

IS A 609 DISPUTE LETTER EFFECTIVE? 32

HOW TO CORRECTLY DISPUTE ERRORS ON YOUR CREDIT REPORT 33

CREDIT DISPUTE TEMPLATES 34

**CHAPTER 4: REMOVING HARD INQUIRIES AND HOW TO
REPAIR AND REBUILD YOUR BAD CREDIT REPORT**............... **48**

HARD INQUIRIES 48

RE-ESTABLISHING YOUR CREDIT 50

YOU'RE IN IT FOR THE LONG HAUL 55

CHAPTER 5: CREDIT REPAIR SECRETS AND STRATEGIES **58**

REVIEWING YOUR CREDIT REPORT 59

THE DISPUTING PROCESS 60

COMMON CREDIT REPORT ERRORS 62

SPOTTING POSSIBLE IDENTITY THEFT 63

CREDITORS CAN HELP.. 64

CREDIT RESCORING... 64

SHOULD YOU USE A CREDIT REPAIR COMPANY?........................ 66

BEWARE OF CREDIT REPAIR SCAMS 66

**CHAPTER 6: THING THAT CRAS AND LAWYERS DON'T WANT
YOU TO KNOW 70**

WHAT CREDITORS LOOK FOR 71

WHAT THE CRAS AND LAWYERS DON'T WANT YOU TO KNOW..... 73

CHAPTER 7: PAYING OFF DEBT 84

START ELIMINATING HIGH-INTEREST DEBTS FIRST 84

KEEP MAKING SMALL PAYMENTS 85

PREVENTIVE MEASURES TO AVOID CREDIT CARD DEBT 85

CHAPTER 8: MINDSET 88

REALIZATION OF YOUR CURRENT MINDSET............................... 88

DEBT IS NOT A BURDEN BUT AN OBSTACLE 89

DON'T FORGET ABOUT GRATITUDE 89

TAKE RESPONSIBILITY FOR YOUR DEBT................................... 90

STOP SEEING DEBT-FREE AS A SOLUTION TO YOUR PROBLEM 91

YOUR GET-OUT-OF-DEBT MINDSET 93

CHAPTER 9: FINANCIAL FREEDOM............................... 98

**CHAPTER 10: PROTECTING AND MONITORING YOUR
CREDIT SCORE 102**

WHAT HAPPENS WITH CREDIT MONITORING?........................... 103

CONCLUSION 108

Introduction

Alot of people know very well that having poor credit can keep us from having a credit card or a loan, but it can also influence us in other ways, such as work promotion or actually getting a job. Employers can use your credit background in hiring decisions—with the government's approval—to decide whether you can manage job responsibilities. The same may also be used by someone who manages their financial responsibilities to handle work responsibilities. The higher your credit rating is, the better chance you have to get a job, get a start-up loan, or grow your company with a loan. Investors or lenders will review your financial status and your credit history before they proceed to grant you a loan. If you can't handle your finances, how can you handle a company's finances? For example, if you sell a product and your credit status is good, the product maker will probably give you the goods to sell, and you will pay for them later.

A bad credit score can prohibit you from renewing a professional license or forbid your home from having cable connections and utilities. You may not possibly post bail for yourself or someone else with a poor credit score if the need arises. Bad credit will adversely affect your life in so many ways if you don't act on it for a long time. For larger payments, higher interest, additional loan points, and bigger premiums, bad credit will cost you a lot of money. For several years, a little negative factor on your credit report can destabilize and haunt you, but having a good credit score can improve your chances of finding better jobs and lower interest rates and fees, and it will help save a lot of money over a long period.

In this book, you can decide what your credit scores carry down and how you can boost your credit score. It will be regarded as outstanding if you can increase your FICO score to over 800, and this book will help you achieve it. It will provide you with a simple guide to attain the required results and will explain how your credit scores can be restored and corrected.

CHAPTER 1:

How to Start and How It Works

Getting Started Cleaning up Your Credit—The Debt Snowball

B efore you can start paying off your debt, it is important to come up with a plan for debt repayment. If you have just one debt to worry about, then the best strategy is to start repaying as much as you can every month. You must keep doing this until you are debt-free.

If you are like many others who are in debt, you might have multiple debts. You must try to develop the best repayment strategy that appeals to you and works well for your financial situation.

One method for repaying your debts is known as the debt snowball. You start repaying your debts in ascending order— starting from the smallest amount to the largest one. As you start clearing small loans, it will give you the motivation to keep going. You can start enjoying your small wins as you make your way to being debt-free.

You must start paying the minimum balance due on all your debts. Once you do this, divert all your extra funds toward the debt with the smallest amount. Once you clear this debt, all the money you spent on this repayment can be diverted towards the next small debt on your list. Keep doing this until you have paid off all your debts. Regardless of whether the interest rates are payable, you must start with the smallest sum due and make your way to the largest one. If you ever played in the snow and made a snowball, you will realize that it keeps collecting more and more snow as the snowball rolls on the ground and becomes bigger. So, every small debt you repay will free up sufficient funds to repay the debt.

Let us assume that you have four debts, and their details are as follows:

- An auto loan repayable at 4.5% for $16,000.
- A student loan repayable at 6.5% for $30,000.
- A personal loan repayable at 8% for $10,000.
- A credit card debt repayable at 21% for $7000.

So, you will start by repaying your credit card debt, which is at $7000, once you repay this diet and have paid the minimum balance due for all the other loans. All the interest that was payable towards the credit card debt can be successfully redirected toward the other loans' payment. You will start with your credit card debt, next to the personal loan, then the auto loan, and finally, the student loan.

This is a great technique to pay your debts, especially if you have several small debts. At times, it can be rather overwhelming and scary when you look at a major debt. It can also be the reason for losing your motivation. To avoid this, when you start clearing the small debts, the number of loans you have to repay will reduce. If you have five loans, and you repay two loans, the figure somehow looks more manageable. Instead of worrying about repaying all the five loans simultaneously, you can concentrate on repaying the smallest ones and then be left with only the major debts.

How the debt snowball method works:

- List the debts from lowest to highest.
- Make minimum payments on all but the smallest debts.
- Follow this process as you clear all your debts.

What Should You Include in Your Debt Snowball?

Your debt snowball should include all non-mortgage debt—a loan that is described as anything else you owe to anyone.

- Car notes.
- Credit card balances.
- Home equity loans.
- Medical bills.
- Payday loans.
- Personal loans.
- Student loans.

When compared to the "avalanche" method, you might end up paying more interest in the long run by using the snowball method. Since the interest rates are never considered in this method, any account that has a higher rate of interest, and a large outstanding balance, will be left towards the end. So, the interest payable will increase.

Is Credit Repair Ethical?

Beware, not all credit repair companies are ethical. Do not fall for scams that promise they can take a bad credit record and turn it around overnight, or maybe those companies would guarantee that they can "force" the credit reporting agencies (abbreviated CRAs and also referred to as credit bureaus, credit reporting bureaus, consumer reporting agencies, or credit reference agencies) to remove all negative—but accurate—information from your credit file immediately. It takes time and cooperation to improve your credit. Trust me when I tell you that a credit repair company cannot push around the large CRAs—never mind ordering them to do things like immediately removing foreclosures or missed payments from their clients' records. Inaccurate information can be easily fixed; however, removing accurate negative information takes a plan and is rarely done overnight. That usually requires filing official disputes and careful negotiations with your creditors.

Some credit repair companies not only misrepresent what they can do for you but also practice illegal or fraudulent ways of trying to improve your credit. They will often reorganize as a nonprofit to get around state and federal laws that govern the industry. If you are desperate enough, you may be tempted to risk some of these illegal actions, but we would not recommend it. Also, be wary of credit repair companies that want to be paid upfront. People have lost hundreds and, in some cases, thousands of dollars to credit repair scams.

The Warning Signs when Choosing a Credit Repair Company

- They recommend that you do not contact credit bureaus directly.
- They do not disclose your legal rights or what you can do yourself.
- They want you to pay upfront based on their verbal promises before they do any work. It is illegal for them to charge you upfront. They can only charge you after they have completed the services they were contracted for.
- They suggest unethical or illegal actions such as making false statements on a loan application, misrepresenting your social security number, or obtaining an EIN (employer identification number) under false pretenses. The use of these tactics could constitute general fraud, civil fraud, mail fraud, wire fraud and get you into a lot of trouble.

Once you receive a copy of your free credit report, take note of your 3-digit credit score, and note any damage to your credit standing due to increased credit utilization, derogatory marks on your report, missed/late payments on your credit cards, closure of old accounts, or recent applications for a new credit card/loan. Sometimes, credit repair can be very simple when it involves fixing disputing mistakes shown on your credit reports with the credit reporting agencies/providers, or an extensive repair when the issue is about identity theft or fundamental financial issues like budgeting. While you seek to rebuild and repair your credit, you want to rectify a poor credit score or pay a company to report and remove any incorrect items from your report. Your credit history is vital to understanding your credit standing. You can file disputes where you observe inaccurate information on your credit report.

CHAPTER 2:

What to Know about Credit

15 Things to Know about Credit

Most people will require credit at some time in their lives. You may want to buy a house, finance a car, or need the money to pay for your studies. There are also times when you require credit for less significant reasons. Some event tickets can only be purchased with a credit card, and you need to own a credit card to rent a vehicle while on holiday. Regardless of your reason for using credit, here are 15 things you should always remember about credit:

1. Credit Does Not Equal Cash

Just because a bank gives some funds to you does not mean that you can go on a spending spree. The money in a credit card or loan is not your money! You do not own that money, and you will need to pay the funds back at some point in time. Be very careful with credit card spending as it can quickly spiral out of control. You should only use your credit card for occasional expenses and only when you know you'll be able to make the required payments by the expected date. It is not advised to use a credit card for daily expenses such as food since it can quickly ruin your budget.

2. Credit Scores and Credit Records Are Not the Same Thing

The credit rating score is a number between 300 and 850 to indicate how well you manage your credit. A number above 700 is considered to be a good score. A credit record (or report) is a detailed document that shows your personal information, past and current credit transactions, any legal cases regarding your finances, and other data. Your credit record will play a role in the calculation of your credit score.

3. A High Score and a Good Record Are essential

A high credit score will help you in your current financial situation and in the future. Any credit application you make will be impacted by your credit history.

A good history of timely payments and credit management provides a sense of security to the lending institution.

Your credit score and credit record provide an indication of the type of person you are when dealing with financial obligations. A good credit score has many benefits.

4. Factors That Affect Your Credit Score

The most used credit scoring model is FICO, which was created by the "Fair Isaac Corporation." The FICO model considers five factors when calculating your credit score. A weighting is applied to each factor depending on its importance. The five factors are payment history, amounts owed to lenders, length of credit history, recent credits and applications, and your credit variety.

5. It Takes Time to Build Good Credit

Credit history is not built overnight, and you need to be patient. It takes at least 6 months to get a credit score, and that will be the benchmark from which to work. Your credit score is dynamic and will change over time. Thus, your credit score will also change, as your responsibilities do. Most people take at least two years to establish a solid, good credit history.

6. Credit Is Not One-Size-Fits-All

Credit is not a universal item that can fit everyone. What works for one person will not necessarily work for another person. This reasoning is what makes a credit score and record necessary. A person who handles credit well should be rewarded for their actions; a person who goes into debt and does not make repayments should face the consequences. You may be able to compare your credit score with another person's credit score, but there are many hidden factors in your credit record that ultimately affect the credits you are offered from banks.

7. Anyone Can Get in Trouble

Money is required in most transactions, and sometimes things get out of hand. You may be managing your money just fine, and then suddenly, you have a pile of bills stacking up on your desk. Sometimes this happens because of a person's poor choices and irresponsible spending. Other times it is simply due to unforeseen circumstances. You should watch your finances very carefully and keep track of your credit so that you don't get into unnecessary trouble.

8. Businesses Tattle-Tale on You

Financial institutions, retail stores, gyms, and even libraries will keep a record of your transactions. The account information is shared by businesses with credit reporting agencies. This information will land up on your credit record and impact your credit score.

9. Your Credit Record Is Important... and Free

You won't know what is reflected in your credit record if you don't check it often. Every person can get one free credit report per year from one of the three main CRAs. You can use the record to check for any mistakes and identify areas to improve your credit score.

10.   Paying Bills Is Not Enough

A credit record isn't just about paying bills on time. Other factors also play a role in your credit score. Paying your bills when due is important, but you need to take additional actions to decrease the amounts you owe and avoid interest. If you pay bills late, it will be reflected in your credit record and affect your credit negatively. So simply making payments (on time or late) will not automatically give you a good credit score.

11. You Can Negotiate and Save

A high credit score puts you in a position of advantage. You can negotiate lower interest rates and reduced security deposits with creditors. Lower financing costs will amount to lots of savings over the long term. Thus, credit can help you save money so that you can use it for other things.

12. There Is Too Much Credit Too

Some credit is good, but it can quickly spiral out of control. Too many credit cards and big loans can make it difficult to meet all your financial obligations. You should keep your budget in mind and be able to pay back your monthly debts.

13. Never Close an Old Credit Card

The credit card you got first is one of the most important ones to hold on to. This will give the most weight to the length of time for which you have had credit. Longer credit history is an advantage that you don't want to lose. Closing your oldest credit card can decrease the age of your credit and subsequently affect your credit score negatively.

14. Other Factors Affect Credit Applications

A credit score and credit record will affect any application you put in for additional financings, such as home loans. Your credit application includes your credit record and other factors to determine your eligibility. Factors such as your income, age, and expenses will play a role in your credit approval.

15. There Are No Shared Credit Scores

A credit score belongs to you as an individual. You cannot share a credit score with someone else. Some people have joint bank accounts or cosigned a loan, but that only means both parties are responsible for making payments.

Your credit score remains your own; however, the actions of the other person/institution can affect your credit score.

What Is a Good Credit Score?

A credit score is a number assigned to you that reflects how well you use credit. When you were attending school, you would receive a report card indicating your performance or grades in a specific subject. Your credit score works just like a report card. A credit score is a grade you receive that indicates your financial performance based on specific factors.

Factors affecting your credit score include payment history, type of credit, age of accounts, the amount of debt you have, and credit applications. Another term you will often see in this book is credit record. A credit record is a list of all the transactions you have made relating to credit. The credit record will inform the credit score; as the record changes, so will your credit score.

There are two models that are used for credit score calculations: "FICO" and "VantageScore." These models are used by most of the lending institutions in the United States and elsewhere across the globe. Both credit scoring methods are improved as new information becomes available. "Fico 9" and "VantageScore 3.0" are the latest models being used by companies.

FICO was created by the "Fair Isaac Corporation" and the most popular credit scoring model across the globe. The company was born in 1956 and has a long history in the financial services sector. VantageScore is a competitor, which was launched in 2006 after being developed by prominent credit reporting agencies—"TransUnion," "Experian," and "Equifax" worked together to create VantageScore, which continues with improvements.

Credit Score Ranges

Fico and VantageScore use a range in which your credit score will fall. Both ranges are from 300 to 850, where a higher score is always better. The ranges differ slightly based on where it places your credit score ranking. The following tables provide an idea of how you may score for each model. The impact your score may have on your financial situation is also shown.

FICO Ratings

The ratings given by FICO are shown below, along with the corresponding credit score:

- 300–579: Very poor
- 580–669: Fair
- 670–739: Good
- 740–799: Very Good
- 800–850: Exceptional

Very Poor: People with a credit score between 300 and 579 are said to have a very poor score; this does not mean that the person is financially poor. It is unlikely that these people will be approved for credit. If an application does succeed, then the applicant may need to pay a deposit or additional fee as security.

Fair: A fair score (580–699) indicates that the person has previously missed payments and does not have a good track record regarding credit. It is possible to improve this score through proper credit control and gain a better record.

Good: People with a good (670–739) credit score can easily obtain credit. Additionally, there is a very small chance for these individuals to suddenly start making poor credit decisions.

Very Good and Exceptional: Most people want to be placed in the category of very good (740–799) or have a score of more than 800 to achieve the rating of exceptional.

These individuals will be offered the best credit card deals from top lending companies. Another advantage of a high credit score is that you will be given low-interest rates when borrowing money.

VantageScore Ratings

The VantageScore ratings are slightly different as seen in the following table:

- 300–499: Very Poor
- 500–600: Poor
- 601–660: Fair
- 661–780: Good
- 781–850: Excellent

VantageScore has an evener distribution of scores across the range. Those with very poor scores (300–499) have almost no chance of being approved for credit. These people will find it difficult to get credits and struggle to improve their credit scores.

People with a poor (500–600) score might get a small amount of credit from some institutions. However, the interest rates will not be good, and some companies may ask for security or large deposits to ensure that they receive their money back. A better position would be a fair score of 601 to 660, as individuals with this rating will get credits more easily but will still have some issues with interest rates being high.

A good credit score (661–780) will ensure that a person is approved for credit and that the person receives competitive interest rates. VantageScore considers anything above 700 to be a great score, and that number falls within a good rating. The best rating is excellent, with scores between 781 and 850. These individuals will receive favorable interest rates and will easily be approved for credits from some of the top lending companies.

Understanding Credit Scores

Your credit score has an impact on credit applications in the future, so you want to get it as high as possible. FICO and VantageScore both indicate that about two-thirds of Americans have a rating of good or better. This statistic shows promise for people who are attempting to build credit. It is not that difficult to do if you are careful with how you use your available credit.

Mortgage providers (the companies providing credit for home loans) indicate that even people with low credit scores can apply for home loans. The biggest difference is that you may not get favorable terms and good interest rates if your credit score is poor. Many lending institutions require a minimum down payment of 10% and additional security if your credit score is below 580. In contrast, a credit score higher than 580 only requires a 3.5% down payment. This example clearly shows why a good credit score is better for people.

Business Credit Scores

Businesses have credit scores just like individuals, but the ratings work in a slightly different manner. You may be operating a business and need a loan to purchase a vehicle or maybe funds for the purposes of the company. It is important to understand the differences between good credit scores for businesses and that of individuals.

The major difference lies in the actual credit scores: Business credit scores fall within a range of 0 to 100. Similar rules still apply, and the closer your business is to a score of 100, the better it will be for your credit applications. A higher score will provide an opportunity for the business to obtain more credit, give access to additional funding, and show your company is in a good financial position. The three main agencies reporting on business credit are "Experian," "Equifax," and "Dun & Bradstreet." Each reporting agency has its own way of calculating a business credit score.

The business credit reporting agencies provide slightly different ratings, even though they all work on a 0–100-point basis. Dun & Bradstreet use their scoring to indicate the possibility of late payment. Businesses with a score between 1 and 49 have a high risk of missing payments, while businesses scoring between 50 and 79 pose a moderate risk, and

companies that have the lowest risk are those that score more than 80.

The Experian score is broken down into more segments: High-risk businesses score from to 10; medium–high-risk score from 11 to 25; medium risk is obtained by businesses with a score between 26 and 50. The segments then become slightly larger. Businesses scoring between 51 and 75 pose a low-medium risk for lenders, and the lowest risk is when a business has a score between 76 and 100.

Equifax works slightly differently. They have one rating system for payment history and another for the likelihood that your business will fail. This book will only look at the one relevant to payment history. Instead of describing the scores in terms of risk, Equifax gives a ranking based on how you pay or how late your payment is to your creditors. Paying your creditors as agreed gives a score between 90 and 100; if you pay in the 30 days following the due date then, your score is between 80 and 89. A score between 60 and 79 is attributed for payment from 3 to 60 days after the due date. Paying creditors from 61 to 90 days late will result in a credit score between 40 and 59, while a score between 20 and 39 is given for payment between days 91 and 120. Any business paying creditors more than 120 days after the due date receives a score from 1 to 19.

Business credit may seem like something unnecessary for some business owners, but there are many reasons to keep your shop in good credit standing, but the major reason is to protect your personal credit score. By having a good business credit score, you will not need to pay business debts out of your personal savings. As soon as business debts get out of control, you may need to pay from private accounts, and this is not a situation you want to be in as you put your individual credit score at risk.

CHAPTER 3:

Section 609 and FCRA

What Is Section 609?

A"609" is known as a "dispute letter," which you would send to your creditor if you saw you were overcharged or unfairly charged. Most people use a 609 letter in order to get the information they feel they should have received. There are several reasons why some information might be kept from you.

A section 609 letter is sent after two main steps. First, you see that the dispute is on your credit report. Second, you have already filed and processed a "debt validation letter." The basis of the letter is that you will use it in order to take unfair charges off your credit report, which will then increase your credit score.

"609 letters" can easily help you delete your bad credit. Other than this, there are a couple of other benefits you will receive from the letter. One of these benefits is that you will obtain your documentation and information because the CRA has to release this information to you. Secondly, you will be able to obtain an accurate credit report, which can definitely help you increase your credit score.

"There are also disadvantages to 609 letters. One of these disadvantages is that collection agencies can add information to your credit history at any time. A second disadvantage is that you still have to repay debt. You cannot use the 609 letters in order to remove the debt that you are obligated to pay. Finally, your creditor can do their own investigation and add the information back into your credit report, even if it was removed." (Irby, 2019).

"One of the reasons section 609 came to be is because 1 out of 5 people state that they have inaccurate information on their credit report." (Black, 2019). At the same time, many people believe that this statistic is actually higher than 20% of Americans.

Is a 609 Dispute Letter Effective?

If you are searching for prototypes of conflict messages, there is probably a reason for that. Consumers normally send grievance letters to large credit reporting agencies (Experian, TransUnion, and Equifax) if they think something is wrong with their credit report. This can happen if they have applied for a loan or other form of credit and they have been informed by the lender that they have been denied due to information in their credit report. When they search their credit report and discover accounts they don't remember; it can also happen. The practical effect of a dispute letter is that it causes the credit reporting agency to investigate and correct any alleged error.

The principle of the 609 dispute letter is that if you petition the credit offices for evidence that they simply cannot provide as part of your dispute letters, such as the initial signed copies of your credit applications or the cashed checks used to pay bills, they would have to delete the contested object because it is unverified. Nevertheless, the FCRA (Fair Credit Reporting Act) entitles us to all of the information in the databases of the credit reporting agencies—not details they do not have in their systems.

While there is plenty of online information about 609 dispute letters, there is no evidence to suggest that any specific letter design is more successful than another. So actually, on the back of a beer napkin, you might apply a credit report claim, and if it's true, then the material has to be changed or deleted. When it comes to your access to an objective credit report, the delivery method is largely irrelevant.

How to Correctly Dispute Errors on Your Credit Report

There are better ways to contest the credit reports than getting copies of dispute documents, and the procedure is really very easy. Next, get copies of your credit reports so you can search them for errors. You have the right to obtain a free copy of your credit reports from "**AnnualCreditReport.com**" once every 12 months. You can also get a free Experian credit report every 30 days.

When you decide that something found on your credit report or accounts is actually false, or if you think the source of the information can no longer validate you, you are protected by law. In those cases, a formal claim should be filed. Specifically, if there are any mistakes in your Experian credit report, you can file the lawsuit online, through good old-fashioned US mail, or by phone. To challenge an item on your Experian credit report via e-mail, print and fill out the "online grievance form," which asks for details to verify your identity and helps you mention the specific items you are disputing and why you believe they are wrong. Then e-mail the form to Experian. The phase of conflict and prosecution cannot take longer than 30 to 45 days, and most investigations are concluded within a few weeks. Once the review process has been concluded by the credit reporting agency, you will be expected to provide written reports within five business days.

Credit Dispute Templates

It is important to remember that disputing positive items on your credit report is not recommended, even if the information is wrong, because it is difficult to get something placed back onto your record once it is removed. Be sure that you truly want something removed from your credit report and know what the effects of doing so will be prior to starting this process. The following is a template for a dispute letter:

Letter 1: Affidavit of Unknown Inquiries

EQUIFAX

P.O. box 740256

ATLANTA GA 30374

My name is John William; my current address is 6767. W Phillips Road, San Jose, CA 78536, SSN: 454-02-9928, Phone: 415-982-3426, Birthdate: 6-5-1981

I checked my credit reports and noticed some inquiries from companies that I did not give consent to access my credit reports; I am very concerned about all activity going on with my credit reports these days. I immediately demand the removal of these inquiries to avoid any confusion as I DID NOT initiate these inquires or give any form of consent electronically, in person, or over the phone. I am fully aware that without a permissible purpose, no entity is allowed to pull my credit unless otherwise noted in section 604 of the FCRA. The following companies did not have permission to request my credit report:

CUDL/FIRST CALIFORNIA ON 6-15-2017

CUDL/NASA FEDERAL CREDIT UNION ON 6-15-2017

LOANME INC 3-14-2016

CBNA on 12-22-2017

I once again demand the removal of these unauthorized inquiries immediately.

(Signature)

THANK YOU

Letter 2: Affidavit of Suspicious Addresses

1-30-2018

ASHLEY WHITE

2221 N ORANGE AVE APT 199

FRESNO CA 93727

PHONE: 559-312-0997

SSN: 555-59-4444

BIRTHDATE: 4-20-1979

EQUIFAX

P.O. box 740256

ATLANTA GA 30374

To whom it may concern:

I recently checked a copy of my credit report and noticed some addresses reporting that do not belong to me or have been obsolete for an extended period of time. For the safety of my information, I hereby request that the following obsolete addresses be deleted from my credit reports immediately.

4488 N white Ave apt 840 Fresno, CA 93722

Brad Kenten

4444 W Brown Ave apt 1027 Fresno CA 93722

13330 E Blue Ave Apt 189 Fresno CA 93706

I have provided my identification card and social security card to verify my identity and current address. Please notify any creditors who may be reporting any unauthorized past accounts that are in connection with these mentioned addresses, as I have exhausted all of my options with the data furnishers.

(Your signature)

This letter is to get a response from the courts to show the CRAs that you have evidence that they cannot legally validate the bankruptcy.

Letter 3: Affidavit of James Robert

U.S BANKRUPTCY COURT

700 STEWART STREET 6301

SEATTLE, WA 98101

RE: BANKRUPTCY (164444423TWD SEATTLE, WA)

To whom it may concern:

My name is James Robert, and my mailing address is 9631 s 2099h CT Kent, WA 99999.

I recently reviewed my credit reports and came upon the above-referenced public record. The credit reporting agencies have been contacted, and they report in their investigation that you furnished or reported to them that the above matter belongs to me. This act may have violated federal and Washington state privacy laws by submitting such information directly to the CRAs Experian, Equifax, and TransUnion via mail, phone, or fax.

I wish to know if your office violated Washington State and federal privacy laws by providing information on the above-referenced matter via phone, fax, or mail to Equifax, Experian, or TransUnion.

Please respond as I have included a self-addressed envelope.

Thank You (your signature)

Letter 4: Affidavit of Erroneous Entry

Dispute letter for bankruptcy to CRAs

1-1-18

JAMES LEE

131 S 208TH CT

KENT WA 98031

Brad Kenten

SSN: 655-88-0000

PHONE: 516-637-5659

BIRTHDATE: 10-29-1985

EXPERIAN

P. O. Box 4500

Allen, TX 75013

RE: BANKRUPTCY (132323993TWD SEATTLE, WA)

To whom it may concern:

My name is James Lee, and my mailing address is 131 s 208th CT Kent, WA 98031.

I recently disputed the entry of bankruptcy that shows on my credit report, which concluded as a verified entry from your CRA. I hereby request your methods of verification; if my request cannot be met, I demand that you delete this entry right away and submit me an updated credit report showing the changes. SEP

Thank you (your signature)

Letter 5: Affidavit for Account Validation

The first letter you send to the credit bureaus for disputes

1-18-2019

TRANSUNION

P.O. BOX 2000

CHESTER PA 19016

To whom it may concern:

My name is John Doe, SSN: 234-76-8989. My current address is 4534. N Folk street Victorville, CA 67378, Phone: 310-672-0929, and I was born on 4-22-1988.

After checking my credit report, I have found a few accounts listed above that I do not recognize. I understand that before any account or information can be furnished to the CRAs, all information and all accounts must be 100% accurate, verifiable, and properly validated. I am not disputing the existence of this debt, but I am denying that I am the responsible debtor. I am also aware that mistakes happen; I believe these accounts can belong to someone else with a similar name or with my information used without my consent, either from the furnisher itself or an individual.

I am demanding physical documents with my signature or any legally binding instruments that can prove my connection to these erroneous entries. Failure to fully verify that these accounts are accurate is a violation of the FCRA and must be removed, or it will continue to damage my ability to obtain additional credit from this point forward.

I hereby demand that the accounts listed above be legally validated or be removed from my credit report immediately.

Thank you (your signature)

Letter 6: Affidavit of Request for Verification Method

The second letter to Credit Bureau if they verified anything

10-22-17

JOSHUA ETHAN

2424 E Dawn Hill way

Merced, CA 93245

SSN: 555-22-3333

Phone: 415-222-9090

Birthdate: 9-29-1987

EQUIFAX

P.O. BOX 740256

ATLANTA GA 30374

To whom it may concern:

I recently submitted a request for investigation on the following accounts, which were determined as verified:

Acct Numbers# (XXXXXXX COLLECTION AGENCY A)

(XXXXXXX COLLECTION AGENCY B)

I submitted enough information for you to carry out a reasonable investigation of my dispute, and you did not investigate this account or account(s) thoroughly enough as you chose to verify the disputed items.

Under section 611 of the FCRA, I hereby request the methods in which you verified these entries. If you cannot provide me with a reasonable reinvestigation and the methods of which you used for verification, please delete these erroneous entries from my credit report. Furthermore, I would like to be presented with all relevant documents pertaining to the disputed entries.

I look forward to resolving this matter.

(Your signature)

Letter 7: Affidavit of Verification Method

Second letter to the collection agency if they verified anything

1-30-2018

JAMES DAVID

1111 N FAIR AVE APT 101

FRESNO CA 93706

PHONE: 559-399-0999

SSN: 555-59-5599

BIRTHDATE: 9-25-1979

EXPERIAN

P. O. BOX 4500

ALLEN, TX 75013

To Whom It May Concern:

I previously disputed this account with your company, and it resulted in you verifying this entry. I am once again demanding validation of this debt for the second time, as I have yet to receive sufficient documentation that legally shows I am responsible for this matter.

In addition to requesting validation, I am formally requesting your method of verification for these entries that I have previously disputed; please supply me with any documentation you may have on file to aid your stance.

If this entry cannot be validated, or if the method of verification cannot be provided to me in a timely manner, I demand that you delete this entry immediately.

Thank you. (your signature)

Letter 8: Affidavit of Fraudulent Information

Letter to CRA for identity theft

10-17-17

HELEN JOHNSON

2525 S CHERRY AVE APT 201

FRESNO, CA 93702

PHONE 559-299-2328

BIRTHDAY 11-30-1990

SOCIAL SECURITY NUMBER 555-89-1111

EQUIFAX CONSUMER

FRAUD DIVISION

P.O. BOX 740256

ATLANTA GA 30374

To whom it may concern:

I am writing this letter to document all of the accounts reported by these furnishers that stem from identity theft. I have read, and I understand every right I have under section 605B and section 609 of the FCRA. Please block the following accounts that are crippling my credit reports as I do not recognize, nor am I responsible for, nor have I received any money or goods from the creation of these unknown accounts.

Please refer to the police report and the ID theft affidavit attached.

1) CBE GROUP (12323239XXXX)

2) LOBEL FINANCIAL (431XXXX)

Please contact each CRA to prevent further charges, activity, or authorizations of any sort regarding my personal information.

Thank you (your signature)

Letter 9: Affidavit of Fraudulent Information

Letter to a lender or collection agency when reporting fraudulent accounts

10-15-17

TARA BROWN

3421 N ROSE AVE APT 211

OAKLAND CA 93766

PHONE 559-369-9999

BIRTHDAY 9-20-1979

SOCIAL SECURITY NUMBER 584-00-0222

MONTGOMERY WARD

RE Account # 722222XXXX

TRANSUNION

P.O. BOX 2000

CHESTER PA 19016

To whom it may concern:

I have recently reviewed my credit reports and found an account listed that I do not recognize. I am informing you today that you are reporting the above-mentioned account that is a result of identity theft, and continuing to report this entry will be in violation of FACTA rules and regulations.

I have never had the account MONTGOMERY WARD 99986518XXXX, and I ask you to cease all reporting and collection activity surrounding this account, which is my right under section 605B of the FCRA. Please refer to the police report.

I ask that this information be blocked and disregarded by your accounting. Thank you for your time, and I will be eagerly waiting for your response.

Thank you (your signature)

CHAPTER 4:

Removing Hard Inquiries and How to Repair and Rebuild Your Bad Credit Report

Hard Inquiries

Whenever a potential lender or a creditor asks to look into your credit report, it raises an inquiry with the CRA in question. The same will reflect in your report. There are 2 types of inquiries, either hard or soft inquiry.

If you apply for a line of credit, and the lender checks your credit report to decide whether you are a potential candidate, then it is a hard inquiry. A hard inquiry will always show up in your credit report. A hard inquiry will affect your overall credit score. If you apply for a mortgage, credit card, auto loan, or any other form of credit, the lender will check your credit report and score. The lender does this with your permission. They will check your credit report with one or all of the major CRAs. Since this inquiry is related to a credit application, they are hard inquiries and will show up in your credit report. And since they show up in your credit report, they will influence your credit score.

Now, let us look at the way in which hard inquiries affect your credit report. If there are too many hard inquiries about your credit report within a short period, then it is a red flag for potential lenders. Hard inquiries, especially multiple ones, can imply that you are looking to open multiple new accounts. If you start opening multiple accounts, it shows that you are in dire need of funds and that your financial position is not that good. It might also mean that you are overspending. So, it harms your credit report as well as your credit score.

You might be thinking that a person might make multiple inquiries about credit because he is shopping for the best deal on loan. Credit rating models do consider this possibility, so most of them will accommodate multiple inquiries made within a short time frame for a line of credit involving a mortgage or a car loan. Numerous inquiries made about a specific credit product will be treated as a single inquiry and will have a relatively smaller effect on your credit report. Usually, you will not be denied credit because of the number of hard inquiries on your credit report. Rather, it is because a hard inquiry is only one of the many factors that are taken into consideration for generating your credit report as well as credit score.

Hard inquiries can stay on your credit report for around two years, but as time passes by, their effect also reduces. Even if you have several hard inquiries within a short period, this cannot be a reason for disqualifying you for credit by a lender. Your credit history, as well as the promptness of payments, are the other factors that are taken into consideration before you are either approved or rejected for a loan.

If the hard inquiry in your credit report is accurate, then you cannot have it removed. However, you can dispute a hard inquiry if it was started without your permission or if there was an error. If you notice a hard inquiry from an unfamiliar lender in your credit report, it is something you must look into immediately. It is often a sign of identity theft. So, if you find any inaccurate hard inquiries in your credit report, then you can raise a dispute about them. Upon investigation, if the CRA realizes that the hard inquiry was indeed inaccurate, then it will be removed from your report. When this happens, its effect will also be removed from your credit score.

Re-Establishing Your Credit

The road to re-establishing your credit can be a bumpy one, especially if you have to start over from scratch. The main thing you want to remember is that you need to have a solid foundation to rebuild your reputation. Several basic guidelines can help you stay on course.

Whatever your goals are, once your credit report has gotten the boost that it needs, the efforts to reestablish your credit should begin with you. While you may have big dreams, you need to recover slowly. You don't want to make a misstep and end up falling back down the rabbit hole again.

Often, after having a rough bout with credit, the tendency is to swear off credit for good. The vow to go strictly cash can be healthy after surviving a difficult time with creditors and bill collectors. However, that is not always a wise decision. In fact, it could make it even more difficult for you later on. You've learned your lesson about bad credit, but you are smarter now, and you know that credit itself is not the bad guy; it's how you use it.

You now have a credit goal, and you know what to do with it. You know how much credit you can charge and still keep your score high, and you know the importance of making timely payments. You have all the tools you need in your arsenal to start your rebuilding campaign.

Step 1: Know How Much Credit You Need

This will give you a general idea of just how much credit you should have.

For this, you need to determine your debt to income ratio. When you are ready to apply for new credit, lenders will look at this percentage to make a final decision on whether or not to give you credit.

The formula for this is simple. Take the total from your list of financial obligations and divide it by your gross monthly income. It will give you the percentage of credit you should have in your arsenal. For example, if your monthly income is $1,500.00 and your total monthly expenses are $800, the formula should look something like this:

$$800/1500 = 53\%$$

The higher this percentage is, the less likely a creditor will be willing to issue you knew credit, even with a good score.

Step 2: Start Small

You may have big dreams, but keep them within realistic boundaries. Remember, you're trying to recover from credit illness. If you had been physically ill to the point where you needed hospitalization, you wouldn't come home from the hospital and automatically resume your same routine. You will build up your strength a little at a time until you are back to the same physical condition you were before.

You should view rebuilding your credit in the same way. Don't look to establish an unsecured bank credit card fresh out of the gate. These are probably the most difficult to get.

When filling out your application, here are a few things to keep in mind to make the process go smoother, and the results will lean more in your favor:

- Do not put in more than three applications for credit in a single month. More than that, and your score will drop.
- Don't add anything to your application that won't benefit you in some way. Some businesses will allow you to make purchases without an established credit, but they will only report to the CRA once you've paid it off. Only put these on your application if you've made regular payments, and you know it will boost your score.
- Only apply to those that will raise your overall credit score.

As the months go by and you are making regular payments, you can begin to increase your purchase amounts little by little. Your creditor will notice that you are spending wisely and will probably drop the need for security behind the card you have and perhaps even increase your limit.

Remember, they make their money by charging interest, so the more money you borrow, the more they can earn. Still, you don't have credit to support them, so maintain self-control and stay within your limits, and your score will naturally increase.

Step 3: Protect what You Have

No matter how much or how little credit you have, never take it for granted. Make sure that you follow the rules, and your credit should stay in good condition.

In regard to revolving credit (credit cards), avoid using them too often. Only spend as much as you can reasonably pay off within a given month. No doubt, you will continue to hit rough patches here and there; even people with good credit need to be prepared. With credit that you use infrequently, make it a habit of making a small purchase from time to time so that the account does not become inactive. Then pay off the total balance immediately when you do.

Establish a rapport with your creditors. That way, if you end up paying late 1 month, you have a friend you can call that can help you to recover quickly. Missing a payment or paying late can be the death knell for a newly recovered credit score; the more friends you have in your corner, the more likely you will come out on top when that happens.

Use automation when you can. We all lead busy lives, and it can be easy for a date to pass by without noticing it. One way to do this is to use modern technology to your advantage by taking advantage of automated payment systems. This will ensure that every payment will be made on time without you even having to worry about it.

There are several ways to do this, and it is pretty easy to make up automatic payment arrangements through any of these plans, but arranging your payments directly with your creditor is probably the fastest and most straightforward way to do it.

A word of caution. If you decide to make this arrangement through your bank, you will always have to make sure that your account has a sufficient balance to make the payment. This can start an ugly domino effect that could threaten to undermine all the efforts you've made to get your credit back on top.

This decision works best for those who have a regular monthly income that they can be sure will be in their bank at the right time. At the end of the day, the main goal is never to be late or miss a payment so you can avoid falling behind and running into a lot more trouble than you bargained for.

You're in It for the Long Haul

When you're under a lot of pressure from collection agencies and creditors, it is easy to think that repairing credit and getting back on track is an emergency, but your credit will be with you for the long haul. There will be some things you won't be able to address immediately, and you will have to wait it out.

Don't rush the process but instead, take your time and be methodical in your approach. Doing so will ensure that the chances of you clearing up your good name are quite good.

Focus on the future, not the immediate present, and you will be driven to make sure that every step you take will be sustainable, and you will be able to establish and maintain your new credit score for years to come.

CHAPTER 5:

Credit Repair Secrets and Strategies

By making your financial goals, setting your budget, finding ways to save money, and requesting a copy of your credit report, you've done your preliminary legwork in trying to get your finances back in order.

Now that all three credit reporting agencies have a copy of your credit report, it's time to roll up your sleeves and tackle the inaccurate information reported on your credit report.

Reviewing Your Credit Report

When you check each of your credit reports, whether it is on the website of the credit reporting agency where you can download it or on a hard copy of your report, which you received in the mail, it is vital that each entry is accurately reported.

When you consider misleading or incorrect information on the credit report, the "Equal Credit Reporting Act" notes that you have the right to dispute the submission with the credit reporting agency. The credit reporting agency has to reexamine the creditor's admission. The inquiry must be concluded within 30 days of receiving the lawsuit message.

If you fail to respond within that time period, the credit reporting agency must delete the entry you are contesting from your credit report. If the creditor replies and the inaccurate entry is corrected, the credit reporting agency will update your credit report. There is also the risk that the borrower can respond to the credit report and not make any changes to it. If you're not happy with your revised credit report, you should write a 100-word paragraph to clarify your side of the story on any of the remaining items on the credit report. This customer statement will then surface any time it appears on your credit report. If you don't want to write a 100-word paragraph on your credit report, you will be able to write another 120-day appeal letter from your most recent credit report.

The Disputing Process

The first thing you need to know is that all three credit reporting agencies have to contest the inaccurate information independently. The disputed appearance may be on all three credit reports or may not. Keep in mind that customers may not belong to all credit reporting agencies.

Even though all three credit reporting agencies have the same information, this does not mean that if an item comes out of one credit report, it will come out of the others. No promise can determine what the outcome will be. That is why you have to refute any inaccurate information about each particular article.

When you access your credit report on the website of the credit reporting agency, you will be able to dispute the incorrect entries online. The site will have boxes to check for inaccuracy alongside an appropriate reason. If you choose to write a personalized message, you can also use the same answers as appropriate. Sample answers would be:

- This is not my account.
- This was not late, as indicated.
- This was not charged off.

- This was paid off in full, as agreed.
- This was not a collection account.
- This is not my bankruptcy, as indicated.
- This is not my tax lien, as indicated.
- This is not my judgment, as indicated.

If you've found more than four entries on your credit report that you need to dispute, don't dispute everything in one letter. Whether you're writing a letter, filling out its form, or answering via the internet, break your disputes. You send or go back every 30 days to the website of the credit reporting agency and challenge up to 4 more things. Don't overshoot that number. If you have to challenge less than 4 things, go ahead and dispute the remaining entries. Extend the spacing of conflicts for 30 days.

On submitting each address, expect to receive a revised credit report about 45 days after you send your letter or disagreement online. If your new credit report has not been issued before, it's time to appeal the second time, so go ahead and mail your second letter or challenge online instead.

Once all the grievance letters have been mailed or posted to the website, and all the revised credit reports have been received, check whether products have been omitted or incomplete. If you need to do the procedure again for the remaining items, space 120 days from your most recent update to the next round of disputes.

Below are something you shouldn't do:

- Alter your identity or try to change it.
- Makeup stories.
- Fail to check that any information is 100% correct.

Below are something you should do:

- Read your emails before sending them. If a letter looks legitimate, credit reporting agencies will believe it has been written by a credit repair service, and they will not investigate the dispute.
- Use your original letterhead (if you do have one).
- Use the appeal form included with the credit report by the credit reporting agency if you want.
- Provide some evidence suggesting that the entry in question is erroneous.
- Include your identification number for all communications listed on the credit report.

Common Credit Report Errors

Note, there could be various mistakes in each of the three credit reports. It is not uncommon to have positive coverage of an account on one article but poor reports on another.

Here are some of the most common credit report errors:

- Listed wrong names, emails, or phone numbers.
- Data that refers to another person with the same name.
- Duplicate details, whether positive or negative, about the same account.
- Records that have negative, or apparently positive information.
- Payable balances on accounts are still on view.
- Delinquent payment reports that were never billed in due time (this indicates wrong credit limits.
- Claims included in the insolvency, which are still due.
- Incorrect activity dates.
- Past-due payments, not payable.
- Court records falsely connected to you, such as convictions and bankruptcy.
- Tax liens, not yours.
- Unprecedented foreclosures.

Spotting Possible Identity Theft

Checking your credit report could also spot potential identity theft. That's why you should inquire at least once a year or every six months for a copy of your credit report.

Things to look for would be:

- Names of accounts and figures that you do not know.
- Loan applications that you don't remember.
- Addresses you didn't live in.
- Poor bosses or tenants' inquiries, you don't know.

Creditors Can Help

Many times, if you have had a long-term account with a creditor, you can contact them directly and explain the error being reported on your credit report.

Ask them to write you a letter with the email and correction. Also, ask them to contact every credit reporting agency that reports this incorrect entry in order to make the correction.

Once the creditor receives a copy of the letter, make a copy of it and attach the letter to the letter of dispute you send. Mail it to the agency for credit reporting and ask them to update their files. Once that is completed, you will be sent back a new credit report by the credit reporting agency.

Credit Rescoring

"Rapid rescoring" is an expedited way of fixing anomalies in the credit file of a customer. The bad news is, you can't do it yourself. A fast rescore dispute process works through borrowers and mortgage brokers, a number of approved registry credit reporting companies, and credit reporting agencies.

If you are a creditor applying for a rescore on your credit report, you would need to provide detailed documents that would be sent to the collateral agencies that are working on your case. "Cash registry" is the system used by cash grantors. The "data archive" gathers the records from the three main credit reporting agencies and has to check the consumer's initial information for a rescore. Once the verification is entered into the program of the repository, a new score will be produced.

The key thing to keep in mind is that a simple rescore can only be temporary. You may be able to close a loan with it, but you must follow through on your credit report with the three main CRAs to ensure it has been removed or corrected. If it reappears, forward the reports immediately to the credit reporting agencies.

The downside of a fast rescore is that you save money without having to contend individually with a credit reporting agency, so that may take longer than 30 days to complete an audit. If the sale of a house or lease depends on your credit score, and you're in a crunch time, the best solution is to rescore easily.

Should You Use a Credit Repair Company?

Using a credit repair company's services is basically hiring a firm to do what you can do for yourself. The process is really without secrets. All the credit repair company does is dispute information on negative entries on your credit report with credit reporting agencies. Most companies may report having agreements with credit reporting agencies or have a secret way to get borrowers to delete unfavorable entries. This is more than likely not true because the credit reporting agencies are regulated by both state and federal laws under the Fair Credit Reporting Act.

The reason some people hire an outsourced credit repair company is that they feel intimidated or have no time to do the work themselves. Before signing up with a credit repair company, there are many steps you need to take. Many businesses operate illegally, and you don't want to get caught in that trap.

Beware of Credit Repair Scams

Sadly, it is easy for people to fall prey to credit repair fraud when they are vulnerable and are going through financial challenges. If you're looking for a repair company for cash, here's how to say if it's a genuine or scam business. Many scam firms may only sign up to take the money and then run from doing their job. This is a list of stuff that should raise a red flag for:

- The company doesn't tell you your rights, and you can do it for free. This should appear in any document the company presents you with.

- The firm advises that you do not explicitly approach any of the three major national credit reporting agencies because if you do, you may learn that the fraudulent firm took your money and that it did nothing.

- The company tells you that even if that information is accurate, it can get rid of all the negative stuff in your credit report. (No one can promise to change anything on your credit report.)

- The company assumes you're trying to create a different "credit identifier." This is known as "file segregation." It is accomplished by filing for the use of an "employer identification number" to create a new credit report instead of the "social security number." That is utterly unconstitutional.

- The firm encourages you to challenge any information contained in your credit report, regardless of the accuracy or timeliness of the material. If the evidence is 100% right, then you have no basis for a disagreement.

Remember, if you are given unlawful advice and follow it while knowing it is illegal, you may be committing fraud, and you will find yourself in lawful hot water.

CHAPTER 6:

Thing that CRAs and Lawyers Don't Want You to Know

T he use of credit has become a cherished American way of life. Due to the increased use of charge accounts—in the form of credit cards and other no-money-down inducements, it became necessary to issue reports concerning the credit history of consumers.

Credit reporting agencies (CRAs) were formed to supply these reports. Credit reporting agencies collect information on credit users and sell it to retailers, banks, credit card companies, finance companies, and other lenders. The information is sold in the form of credit reports, and it contains an evaluation mark of positive, negative, or neutral.

CRAs freely exchange information with each other, about almost every adult in this country who has ever requested credit. They pass information to other bureaus when people move, for example. If you have a good credit record in your hometown, you can get credit anywhere in the United States. CRAs keep on file information supplied over time by your creditors, but they do not rate how good or bad credit risk is; they do not make any judgment on your ability to repay a loan. It is up to the potential creditor requesting the file to decide whether to grant you credit. The three major national credit reporting agencies maintaining your credit records. All three work independently of each other in gathering information about you. They have vast databases that track the credit history of several hundred million people around the world.

Experian is the largest with $4.7 billion in revenues in 2013. Equifax, with $1.9 billion in revenue, is the oldest of the three agencies and maintains information on over 400 million credit holders worldwide. TransUnion is the third-largest CRA in the country, with $1.1 billion in revenues.

What Creditors Look for

In order to establish a good credit reputation, you need a thorough understanding of the credit game. The theory most often used in determining your creditworthiness is sometimes referred to as the three C's of credit.

These three C's are:

Character

Character is determined by the way you have handled your transactions in the past. Creditors will look at such things as how much you owe, how often you borrow, and how reliably you have repaid past debts. They also consider how long you have worked in your present job, residence at your present address, and whether you own or rent.

Capacity

This reflects your financial ability to repay your loan. Creditors will ask you to furnish information about your employment: Your occupation, the length of time you have held this or the last job, and how much you earn.

Capital

Capital refers to your assets, which can serve as collateral for your loan. The credit grantor wants to know what valuable property or money other than your regular income could be used to secure your loan. Your assets include your house, jewelry, car, stocks and bonds, savings, and other valuables.

Credit grantors or lenders use different combinations of these facts in reaching their decisions. Each credit grantor extends credit based on their own policies and standards. One creditor may find you to be creditworthy, while another may deny you credit. If you do not have credit experience (character), you may still be granted credit on the basis of your capital and capacity until you establish a solid credit reputation.

What the CRAs and Lawyers Don't Want You to Know

1. You Disputed the Error Only with the Furnisher

If you know that the lender misreports your details to the CRA, it can seem quicker to fully circumvent the credit reporting agency and deal just with the lender. Don't do it.

CRAs used to rely heavily on a supplier's investigation to validate a mistake. However, in a 2015 settlement with the state of New York, the three major CRAs agreed to investigate disputes more closely if customers presented facts supporting their argument, and an initial analysis checked the errors without proposing any improvements.

2. You've Lost Evidence

"If you send dispute after dispute to credit reporting agencies and keep going nowhere, the next best move could be to sue the CRA," according to experts. (You can even make a report to the CRA.)

You're not going to get far in your lawsuit, though, if you haven't saved facts to show that the error is true—and you've been seriously harmed, as consumer lawyers say.

In a variety of court cases reviewed by "**CreditCards.com**," many people have lost the opportunity to plead the case before a jury because they have not saved enough proof that could be used in court to show that they have been wronged.

Instead, their case was referred to the summary judgment at the request of the CRA or the information supplier, which led to a decision by a judge rather than a jury trial.

In order to bring a case before a summary judgment and have a jury to hear the argument—which gives you the best chance of winning the case—you will have to provide proof demonstrating that there is a reasonable discrepancy on what happened to the dispute and how the outcome adversely impacted you.

This involves saving records, such as a certified mail receipt, which indicates that the CRA has processed your dispute.

"The big three regularly lose or pretend to lose customer correspondence," says Leonard Bennett, a consumer advocate with "Consumer Litigation Associates," in "Newport News," Virginia.

"If a prospective lender has told you that a negative entry has led to rejection or approval at a higher interest rate, get the name and title of the lender's representative telling you that, and get something from them in writing."

It also involves storing all of your financial paperwork, including any credit denials you have got. "Those denials of credit letters are evidence that the customer could have been affected by errors in the credit report."

"Saving your denial of credit letters may also help if you need to contest the creditor's behavior for other reasons," says Cary Flitter, a consumer lawyer and law professor in Philadelphia.

Providing further documentation would also make it more likely that credit bureau would immediately correct the mistake when you challenge it, helping you to avoid lengthy court proceedings.

Credit reporting agencies used to discard or refuse to give evidence to lenders, as claim experts. However, since 2013, credit reporting agencies have faced increased oversight from the "Consumer Financial Protection Bureau" and State Attorney Generals, promising to revise their dispute procedures and to take facts more seriously.

For example, as a result of the 2015 agreement with the State of New York, employees of the CRAs are now expected to check mistakes by using the facts they have submitted, rather than relying on automated dispute processes.

Employees can also speed up inquiries if a mistake includes identity theft, fraud, or mixed files. They have to hand out supporting documents to specially qualified personnel. Starting in June 2018, CRAs will not be able to deny your dispute if you have already submitted a dispute in the last three years.

These laws do not—and will not—apply; however, if you send your dispute through a credit repair company rather than personally, be sure to supply your details yourself.

3. You Didn't Include Enough Information in Your Dispute

When contesting credit report mistakes, people often opt for convenience and file a lawsuit online or by phone.

Credit reporting agencies are actively promoting this brevity by selling on their websites how convenient it is to use their online dispute systems, which gives you barely enough space to make a brief statement on your dispute.

Consumer lawyers, however, warn that using the form given by the credit bureau—without the inclusion of extra documentation or a longer letter detailing your conflict—could cost you the case if you later had to bring the credit bureau to court.

CRAs now allows you to attach additional facts to your online dispute explicitly.

However, instead of sending a detailed letter to the CRAs, experts recommend that you:

- Give explanations as to why the information in the study is inaccurate.
- Provide proof to show the error.

By sending the documentation with your letter (and making copies of your files), you make it much harder for the CRA to later argue that the mistake was your fault because you didn't send enough proof, as consumer lawyers say.

Similarly, experts suggest that you send identical copies to the lender linked to the mistake for the same purpose. CRAs will forward any evidence you attach to your dispute, including any additional letters you compose describing your dispute. But it could also be a great idea to send a separate letter to the data providers, just in case.

Lenders and other data providers have also been warned by the Consumer Financial Protection Bureau that they need to examine consumer disputes more closely than they have in the past.

In addition, the 2015 agreement with the state of New York allows credit bureaus to track data providers more vigorously and to penalize providers that do not follow correct procedures. Therefore, the data provider will also have more motivation to adequately examine the conflict if you provide them with ample evidence to believe that the information they provide is inaccurate.

4. You also Missed the Terms of the Agreement with the CRA

If you recently ordered a credit report online or approved a "free report" from one of the three major CRAs, you probably skipped the terms at the bottom of the web page. A lot of people do.

This is a huge mistake. Some credit reporting agencies, such as TransUnion, also have an arbitration provision in their terms of service.

This means that if you buy your credit report online and notice a mistake, you can still contest the mistake. However, if you do not agree with how the CRA handled the dispute and would like to take 'office to court,' the CRA could attempt to legally enforce the arbitration clause and compel you to give up your right to plead your case before a jury takes part in a class-action suit against them.

That can make it even more difficult to prove your case and win significant damage (money paid as compensation) if you have been financially wronged, as experts claim.

In the arbitration proceedings, the complaint will be dealt with by an individual arbitrator appointed by the arbitration association selected by the CRA, and it will be up to the arbitrator to determine the case. If you do not accept the arbitrator's ruling, you are not entitled to appeal.

If you receive a credit report from an office that enforces an arbitration clause, be sure to send an opt-out letter to the CRA within 30 to 60 days of receipt of the report, depending on the arrangement of the company.

Depending on the placement clause on the website of the CRA, you will also be able to claim that the arbitration clause is not legally enforceable because it was not clear that it applied to the credit report you purchased.

The U.S. in March 2016: The Court of Appeals held that the TransUnion arbitration provision found in the website service agreement was not legally enforceable because the office had failed to make it clear to customers that the acquisition of a TransUnion credit score automatically committed them to arbitration. However, it would be best for you to opt-out of the arbitration arrangement entirely.

Besides, don't forget to reexamine the terms of the CRA if you're working with them again in the future—even if you haven't seen an arbitration clause the last time you've searched their terms.

Currently, some credit reporting agencies are not requiring customers to arbitrate on concerns about the dispute process. For example, Equifax and Experian now state in their terms of service that the arbitration provisions of the firms do not extend to the Fair Credit Reporting Act cases. However, this could change if the CRA continues to feel less pressure from regulators and activists. The heightened pressure exerted by the CRAs under the Obama administration has already begun to decline. For example, in November 2017, the Trump administration needed a "Consumer Financial Protection Bureau (CFPB)" regulation that would have prohibited CRAs and other financial institutions from applying arbitration clauses that would prohibit individuals from joining together in class-action suits.

Under new leadership, the CFPB demonstrated less ability to control financial services firms actively. As a result, certain

CRAs might feel motivated to reintroduce wider arbitration agreements.

Irrespective of the political climate, it's still a good idea to have a habit of scanning words any time you get a credit report or launch an online conflict.

5. You Listened to a Debt Collector

You can't challenge the correct facts about your credit reports and expect the CRAs to delete it. You can, however, hold CRAs liable under the Equal Credit Reporting Act if they fail to comply with the time limit on your debt.

Negative information is required by law to drop the report after 7 years. Insolvency can remain on your report for up to 10 years.

If you see a debt that is real and has been in it for more than 7 years, you can challenge the debt to the CRAs and demand that it be canceled. You may also fight back against a debt collector who threatens to sue you for a debt if it has reached its time limit.

The legal expiration date on the debt should allow you the right to defend any case brought after the time limit has expired. But that tactic only works if you didn't unintentionally reinforce your debt after talking to a debt collector, says Paul Stephens, "Privacy and Advocacy Director at Privacy Rights Clearinghouse."

"There's a huge problem with this particular topic," says Stephens. Debt collectors also sell accounts to one another, and often debt collectors disclose incorrect schedules, causing the debt to be recorded longer than it should be.

"That's what we call debt re-engineering," he says. This does not happen under the Equal Credit Reporting Act, and you have the right to fight against it.

However, if you receive a debt collector call and agree to pay part of the unpaid debt, you may theoretically restart the debt restriction clock and weaken your ability to fight back effectively.

"Debt collectors will keep calling you and hounding you," Stephens says. *"They can get you at a fragile or vulnerable moment, and at that point of depression, you can make a commitment to enter into a payment plan or possibly accept the debt."*

At that point, the debt collector will sue you—and possibly win a judgment against you—for a debt that you should have been able to write off from your credit history for good.

CHAPTER 7:

Paying off Debt

Start Eliminating High-Interest Debts First

Whenyou are trying to eliminate your credit card debt, the biggest obstacle that will stand in your way is the ones that carry a very high rate of interest. Sometimes, the rate of interest can even be in double digits, sometimes as high as 22%. In that case, paying it off can be a really difficult task. But the reason why I am asking you to start eliminating them first is that when you have finally cleared these debts, you will have a greater amount of money left in your hands at the end of each month. Another thing that you could do, but only if you have enough credit available, is to apply for a new credit card. But this should be a zero-interest one. Once you get it, transfer the balance to eliminate the high-interest debts. Yes, I know that some of you might be thinking that applying for another credit card is not a sensible thing to do, and that is why I will be asking you to get it only if you think you have enough self-restraint to not buy a bunch of stuff that you don't need.

Keep Making Small Payments

Quite contrary to the technique I mentioned above is another technique which is called the snowflake technique. With this process, you will be making small payments towards your debt every time you get some extra cash in your hands. Whatever payment you are making, it does not matter as long as you keep paying. You can pay $10, or you can pay $20, but at the end of the year, you will find that you have reduced about $1000 simply by paying such small amounts almost every day, even if you are paying $2 on any day. People often ignore this method, thinking that it will be only small amounts, but you should not make the mistake of overlooking these small amounts, as they have quite some power in them. When you are making these small payments, it would feel as if they are not even leaving any dent, but with time, they will sum up and cause a considerable effect on your debt.

Preventive Measures to Avoid Credit Card Debt

Have an Emergency Fund

Think about a situation when you have encountered a problem that requires you to spend a lot of money; for example, a car repair, a job loss, or medical emergencies. In such a situation, what you need is an emergency fund—but people use credit cards for help when they don't have an emergency fund. But why arrive at such a situation when you can build an emergency fund that will cover at least six months' expenses. If you are finding it difficult to come up with a huge amount, then start by accumulating $500 and then work your way up to $1000. A fund of this size will help you to figure out any small expenses that crop up overnight. Take your time to build your emergency fund so that you do not have to rely on debt ever.

Buy only Things that You Can Afford

When you have a credit card in your hands, it can get really tempting, and you may start buying whatever you think you want. But take a step back and think about whether you can really afford that item if you did not have a credit card. If not, then don't buy it now. Make a goal to save the money required for purchasing that item instead of buying it on credit.

Don't Transfer Balance If Not Necessary

Some people have this habit of clearing their balance with a higher credit card but such, repeated balance transferring can actually backfire on you. When you keep transferring balanced without keeping track of your activities, you might end up with an ever-increasing balance, and you will also have to clear the fee requirements for all those transfers.

Try Not Taking out a Cash Advance

Sometimes, you may be in the moment, and you were not thinking clearly so you decide to take a cash advance. But you have to remember and remind yourself that a cash advance comes with very hefty transaction fees, and you are not even going to get a grace period in which you can avoid the charges. Moreover, you will have to realize that you are getting into credit card debt if you have started making cash advances. The moment you see it happening, you will have to start working on that emergency fund and also tweak your budget.

Lastly, I would like to say that no matter how many measures you take, try avoiding increasing your credit cards unnecessarily because the more the number of credit cards, the more you will have to stop yourself from overspending.

CHAPTER 8:

Mindset

Realization of Your Current Mindset

B efore you start to make any changes, you need to know where your mindset is at the moment. Think of how you feel when you ponder about your credit card debt, as this will tell you more about your mindset than you might realize.

If you are like most people, you feel frustrated about your current situation.

How you got into credit card debt will depend on what you are saying to yourself.

For example, you might be angry or blame yourself for getting into debt. You might ask yourself why you allowed this situation to happen.

No matter what you notice about your current mindset, you need to accept it and understand why you feel this way. You also need to understand that it is okay for you to feel like this, as it will help you reach the get-out-of-debt mindset.

Debt Is Not a Burden But an Obstacle

There is a difference between a burden and an obstacle. When you have a burden, you have to deal with it; there is no way around it. However, there is a way around an obstacle. Therefore, you need to look at debt as an obstacle. It is something that you can overcome with the right steps. It is also something that you can keep yourself from getting into again.

Take a moment to think of ways that you can work toward erasing your credit card debt as an obstacle. For example, if you have a $75 minimum monthly payment that you have been doing, how much is going toward interest and fees? If you notice that this amount is $35, see what you can do in order to increase your monthly payment to $110. This will allow you to pay more than your minimum payment. More importantly, it will also allow you to put $75 toward your balance, with half of your amount toward fees and the other half toward your balance.

Don't Forget about Gratitude

Debt can cause us to become resentful. We often see other people enjoy the luxuries of life, whether it is by purchasing a new vehicle or going on a vacation. You might even feel resentful because they are able to afford new clothes. One of the best ways to get out of the negative mindset that is attached to credit card debt is to let go of your resentment and focus on gratitude.

Look around your home to see all the wonderful items that you own. Try to think about how lucky you are when it comes to your family, friends, and everyone else who is in your life. You don't always need to focus on the bigger things; sometimes, looking at the smaller moments is just as helpful. For example, you may feel gratitude when your child gives you a smile while they are playing quietly with their toys.

If you struggle with gratitude, one of the best techniques is writing down what you are grateful for at the end of every day. Find a journal and discuss everything that made you feel positive. You can also discuss what bad things happened, but try to find a way you can learn from them or turn them into something a little positive.

Take Responsibility for Your Debt

There is a big difference between blaming yourself for your credit card debt and taking responsibility for it. The biggest difference is what type of mindset you are in. For instance, if you are asking yourself how you could have been so dumb to allow yourself to obtain so many credit cards, you are blaming yourself for what happened. Instead, you need to take responsibility, which means you should try saying to yourself something like, "I know I got myself into credit card debt because I took out too many credit cards. Now, how can I start to pay off my credit card debt?"

Taking responsibility helps you have the right mindset because it helps you realize that even though you made a mistake, you understand the error and are ready to solve the problem. On top of this, you should always look at how you can keep yourself from making the same mistake again. No matter how you get yourself out of credit card debt, they are always going to be tempting.

Stop Seeing Debt-Free as a Solution to Your Problem

Another step you want to take to prepare yourself for your mindset of getting out of debt is to stop looking at becoming debt-free as the solution to your problem. The reality is that there is probably more than one reason why you are in debt. While you want to avoid blaming yourself, you also need to take responsibility for your mistakes.

Therefore, write down all the ways that you can become free of debt. This might mean that you should close all your credit cards and work on a plan to pay them off in a timely manner, or it may also mean that you should get a second job to help pay off your debt quickly. Instead of thinking about becoming debt-free as the only solution, you need to think of it as the outcome. You need to make becoming debt-free or having financial freedom be your ultimate goal. You should work on coming up with a series of steps that will help you reach your goal. For example, let's assume that you're a college student who has opened up five credit cards. You are soon graduating and know that you need to start paying off all your smaller debts because you will be paying off student loans in the very near future. Therefore, you decide that one of your best options is to pay off your credit cards and no longer allow yourself to use them. Therefore, you work to think about how you can pay off your five credit cards in a single year.

Another example, you think about all the tips you receive from your job as a waitress. Typically, you bring home anywhere from $100 to $300, depending on the night and how busy it is. You realize that you can put all your tip money toward paying off your credit cards. This will allow you to pay off your debt faster. After doing the math, you realize that all your credit cards will be paid off in full by the time your student loans will begin requiring payment. Through your planning, you started to see becoming debt-free from credit cards as your outcome instead of your solution. By doing this, you were able to come up with a logical solution that works, provided that you are able to follow it over the course of the year.

Your Get-out-of-Debt Mindset

Set a Game Plan and Stick to It

You need to create goals and create your plan of action to get out of debt. While you don't have to write your plan down, this is always a good idea as it will help you remain focused on what you need to do. For example, you know that you have five credit cards which are all maxed out. In fact, you are close to going over the limit on most of them, which will make the credit card company charge you an over-the-limit fee. You realize that this will only create a larger amount of credit card debt. Therefore, you decide that you need to pay more than your minimum payment on these credit cards first.

Reframe Your Thoughts

Another major step for your mindset to get out of debt is to turn your negative thoughts into positive ones. This is one of the biggest reasons why you want to become grateful for what you have in life, including your credit card debt. Even though this might be hard to do right now, it is important to realize that this is a life lesson you are learning. In fact, by taking control of your credit card debt, you will be able to take control of your budget and reach financial freedom. Furthermore, the more negative you are, the less likely you will be to follow your goals and your budget.

Write down a List of Reasons to Get out of Debt

Getting out of credit card debt is not going to be easy. In fact, you will need to take steps to keep yourself focused as there will be times when you will feel frustrated or will lack confidence in getting out of debt. One of the ways to overcome this is by writing down a list of reasons for wanting to get out of debt. This list can include anything that comes to your mind. For example, you might write that you want to own a home one day. You might also state that you want to be debt-free within two years. Another reason might be your children will be going to college starting in five years, and you want to be able to help them. It doesn't matter what your reasons are; what really matters is that they are your reasons for getting out of debt.

Realize that People Depend on You

If you have a family, you will want to think about all the people who depend on you for your income. It is a lot easier to be able to go out and buy diapers, groceries, and any other household items you need when you don't have to worry about what debt you are getting into. Instead, you can pay through your debit card or with cash without having to worry about the purchase again.

Set up Automatic Payments

Every credit card company will allow you to set up automatic payments through their website. Some will even set up automatic payments while over the phone. Whatever you need to do, take time to set up these payments. This will help you make sure that these bills are getting paid. The trick is that you want to refrain from canceling or postponing your automatic payments, as this is typically an option. Again, this is something that you can put into your plan to become less likely to cancel the automatic payments.

Find Ways to Keep You Motivated

While you are creating your get-out-of-debt plan, you want to include ways that will help you stay motivated. Perhaps this means checking your progress every other month to see how much your credit card debt has gone down. For example, if you have five credit cards and you are paying $100 on them every month, you will see they have gone down close to $200 every two months. If you add this up, you have decreased your total credit card debt by $1,000. You can decide to track your progress through a spreadsheet on your computer or via a journal. Note the amount you owe when you pay and then notice the new amount the next time you make a payment.

Know that You Can Do It

Sometimes we struggle to follow through with our debt-free plan because we feel like we can't achieve it. It is important to note that there will be times you feel this way. There will be moments when you feel like you can't continue focusing on paying off your debt. You might look and see that you still have two years of credit card debt to pay off and that your other bills continue to pile up.

Establish a Reward System

The fact is that you will find yourself struggling to maintain your mindset of getting out of debt from time to time. This might not be because you want to purchase something that you can't afford, but rather it may be because you find yourself getting tired of seeing how much money you owe toward credit cards.

CHAPTER 9:

Financial Freedom

Now, if you already have your credit cards and you have incurred expenses greater than your income, of course, the monthly payments will be difficult to cover without affecting the budget necessary for the maintenance of your basic expenses, which are vital to your livelihood. It is at this moment that you will need to design a plan to get out of the debts that afflict you so that they do not affect your requirements and you can improve your credit history.

In that sense, you can consider the following suggestions if you want to get out of your credit card debt:

You should suspend the use of credit cards, especially those that demand higher interest payments. Do not hesitate to use scissors to cut them for safety and freedom; it is better not to have what will not be used.

Of course, you should not stop paying the monthly installment of your credit cards and if necessary to achieve this, go to the financial and banking agencies to request the renegotiation of the debt in order to agree on monthly payments that can amortize the debt.

If you have extensions of your credit cards, you must eliminate the temporary or definitive use of those credit cards to your relatives or associates; all this will benefit your credit history.

You must give priority to your expenses, and if necessary, only allow yourself to have the credit cards that yield greater benefits so you can get offers in cases of having to travel exclusively for work.

Since you cannot finance your card payments on time and your income does not allow it, opt for alternative jobs that allow you to earn new income. Don't make the mistake of incurring new debts to pay the ones you already have.

The sumptuous leisure or recreation expenses that you usually add to the credit on your cards should be suspended for the duration of the credit recovery or payment of delinquent debts.

When undertaking to use of the credit cards again, investigate and inform yourself properly of the interest rate and the taxes that are required. Then use those that are most useful for you—at this point, always less is more.

The commitment you make to your credit history is yours alone, and it is your responsibility, so don't think that there will be magic solutions to get you out of the excesses committed.

Remember, the recovery of your credit history will depend on the degree of commitment you have to control your finances. You must program your expenses, making a budget where you can, according to your income, distribute the payments of your expenses.

If you delegate this function, you will not change your consumption habits and, therefore, you will continue with uncontrolled expenses that put you at risk and prevent you from recovering your credit history. Above all, don't pay a credit repair agency to do the work that is solely your responsibility. These agencies often use illegal or unreliable tactics—maybe you could end up having more problems than benefits.

Limit the use and opening of accounts in stores as this affects your credit rating negatively in the short, medium, and long term. Use only credit cards obtained at financial and banking agencies of wide credibility. Also, consider not using more than one-third of your line of credit unless you're sure you can afford to pay it in full that same month. Do not leave debts for the next few months—thinking that you will be able to pay it with an income that is not fixed.

Many companies pretend to offer free credit reports but charge for their monitoring services. These companies encourage you to sign up for a free report, ask for your credit card, and automatically switch you to a paid service after a trial period. Therefore, if you do not cancel your subscription within this period, you will be charged every month for their services.

If you need specific information about local credit reporting agencies or other aspects of credit ratings where you live, check with the relevant CRAs in your country.

The financial reality is changing in each country, and, of course, the economic conditions in some countries can sometimes be unfavorable, especially for micro and small business as well as entrepreneurs. As they cannot access bank loans, they are forced to resort to informal lenders, weakening their financial and economic capacity, because the interest rates they charge tend to rise steadily, often exceeding the rates of return generated by their businesses, so instead of helping to grow, those informal lenders ended up decapitalizing the credit users. In this case, it is preferable to turn to trusted individuals or state entities for credit support or refinancing.

CHAPTER 10:

Protecting and Monitoring Your Credit Score

In addition to fraud alerts and credit freezes, you can invest in credit monitoring to protect your credit. It means monitoring and inspecting your credit history, as shown in your credit report. In the end, it is all about your credit report and, more importantly, unexpected changes to your credit report. A credit monitoring service provides this monitoring service for you (for a fee, of course). Most credit monitoring services report that they monitor and track your credit report daily.

What Happens with Credit Monitoring?

Once you sign up with a credit monitoring company, they pull all your information from all three credit reporting agencies and typically ask if you are in the process of applying for new credit. Often, they will ask you to check the credit report and verify the information. Of course, they will want to know about any activity you consider suspicious. Now, your new credit monitoring service has a baseline or starting point. Any changes to your credit report going forward could be flagged as possibly fraudulent. Depending on the options available and the monitoring plan you chose, you will be alerted of any suspicious activity that could affect your credit report.

The credit monitoring companies typically are on the alert for:

- New credit inquiries.
- Delinquencies.
- Negative information that suddenly shows up.
- Employment changes.
- New credit accounts.
- Increased credit lines at existing accounts.
- Other changes to your credit report that could be considered a red flag for identity theft.

You should note that one reason why credit monitoring services have become so popular lately is that their alerts for suspicious activity on your credit report are viewed as a counter to identity theft. Some credit monitoring companies even promote their services with this claim.

Advantages

Constant Tracking: All of your credit reports are constantly tracked. Depending on your choice of credit monitoring companies and plans, this monitoring could be daily or weekly.

Increased Knowledge: It is about your own credit. During the time you use a credit monitoring service, you will gain an incredibly valuable firsthand knowledge of how personal credit actually works. Simply by watching the reports provided by your credit monitoring service, you will see in real-time how your credit report changes. You will see how even small actions on your part can have a sizeable effect on your credit score. For example, you can watch your credit score drop right after you applied for four different department store credit cards.

It Does not Cost but Saves: Yes, this is a tired old cliché, yet here it truly works. Consider it this way: Suppose you use your new knowledge to note how your personal credit works, how small things affect your credit score, and what sort of things can help you get a better loan rate. Really, it is that easy. For example, let us say you use your newfound credit wisdom to raise your credit score by 75 points. Then, you refinance your home and get a lower interest rate that saves you hundreds of dollars a month or thousands of dollars over the term of your mortgage.

Identity Theft Protection: Since your credit report is under constant scrutiny, detection of possible fraudulent activity happens much faster. The credit monitoring service helps you both detect and minimize damage from the malicious use of your personal financial information. Additionally, many credit monitoring companies offer legal protections and financial reimbursements. These reimbursements can range from $25,000 to $1,000,000. Surely you have seen the advertisements with the big-name credit monitoring service offering their one-million-dollar guarantee.

Faster Resolution of Errors: Should you spot an error on one of your many reports sent to you by your credit monitoring service, then most of them will assist you in correcting the error.

No More Guesswork: Since you are paying for professional credit monitoring, you do not have to guess what is going on with your credit score or your credit report. Additionally, since your credit monitoring service will alert you for any suspicious activities, you are always aware of what is happening with your credit.

Less Hassle for You: Yes, credit monitoring can be done by yourself, as will be explained shortly. However, paying for a credit monitoring service eliminates one more thing for you to do.

Disadvantages

Price: Of course, all of the services provided by credit monitoring companies come at a price. Price is one common complaint against credit monitoring companies. Each company sets its own pricing structure. Also, many of them offer different levels of service at different price points.

Information Disparity: The information available from one credit monitoring service can be vastly different from another credit monitoring service. Make sure you know what you are paying for when you sign up for a credit monitoring plan.

Cancellation Issues: There are various reports (complaints) from past customers of some credit monitoring services regarding the difficulty encountered in cancelling the service.

Micromanagement Time Wastes: Because your new credit monitoring service provides you with frequent reports and analysis, you may end up trying to micromanage your credit score.

This micromanagement could end up costing you a lot of time with few if any substantive changes to your credit score.

False Sense of Security: Since you are paying for a credit monitoring service, the tendency is to fall into the trap of believing it is what you need to do to protect yourself. Identity theft protection involves additional areas beyond your credit report, which you still need to monitor.

It Cannot Do it as Fast as You Might Want: It is not yet possible to monitor a person's credit history on a real-time basis. For one, many creditors only report information on existing clients weekly or even monthly.

It is not the Final Solution: Even the very best credit monitoring service is not capable of fully identifying all fraudulent activities. Consider that there are many credit details that are never even reported to a credit reporting agency.

Conclusion

C redit is significant for anybody's accounts. It gives an individual history and reputation of their budgetary history. With credit, individuals can fund things like a house or a vehicle. At whatever point an individual has credit, it is significant that they use it shrewdly. A decent record as a consumer will empower you to get low financing costs on credits, just as you can get more cash. There are various things that you should remember when utilizing credit. You should do things like taking care of tabs on schedule, checking the announcements of those tabs, checking your credit reports, and maintaining a strategic distance from the base installment propensity.

Dealing with your record is significant on the off chance that you need to ensure that you can acquire enough cash to purchase a house or a vehicle. It will likewise enable you to get the most minimal loan costs, which sets aside cash for you. At whatever point you are hoping to deal with your credit, it will be imperative to ensure that you spend a sum that you can stand to pay back as you take care of the tabs on your schedule. This will enable you to build up and keep up a decent credit record.

As you have read, after taking a fall, there are so many ways for you to rebuild and jump back into the credit arena. The problem people tend to face after recovering is that there is always that latent desire to return to old habits. The idea that can go through your head when you're debating with yourself about whether or not making a purchase may be, "Just one time; I'll just use my credit card." Don't do it!

You've worked hard with resettling and restoring your reputation to this level. It wasn't done overnight, but now you're in a position where you should be worry-free.

Holding the accounts and finances in order is a cycle that continues for life. Regarding dieting, they say it's a change in lifestyle and the same goes for our finances. Not only will you feel good about your condition by changing your lifestyle and living within your means, but you can also serve as an example to your family and friends. Children learn from how their parents handle their finances. Chances are, if you're a good money planner, your kids will also be when they're adults. Even if you've fallen on hard times, the kids will see how you've picked yourself up.

The main thing to take away from this book is to make sure you've got a workable budget. This cannot be put enough emphasis on. If your budget is getting out of your control and you do not keep track of what's going in and out, then it is going to set you off, at the very least. It is a new practice worth learning about.

There are ever-changing new laws and regulations. Staying on top of any new changes is part of your new financial life. Please read the documents the bank and credit card firms are issuing. Even the small fine print you can barely read contains details that can change your credit terms and save you more money.

You can't be overly careful with your personal identification in today's society. It's too sad that we need to watch for unscrupulous people who want to exploit our identities and use them in all the wrong ways. At all times, be on the lookout to defend yourself and your identity.

Go ahead and give yourself a pat on your back. You deserve this. You're back on your feet now, and you've learned from your mistakes. It's time to start working towards your milestones.

CPSIA information can be obtained
at www.ICGtesting.com
Printed in the USA
BVHW041747190521
607713BV00015B/2078